DESSERTS

DESSERTS

PERFECTLY PREPARED TO ENJOY EVERY DAY

This edition published in 2012
LOVE FOOD is an imprint of Parragon Books Ltd

Parragon
Chartist House
15–17 Trim Street
Bath, BA1 1HA, UK

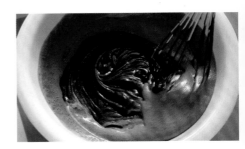

ISBN: 978-1-78186-723-5

Printed in China

Concept: Patrik Jaros & Günter Beer
Recipes and food styling: Patrik Jaros www.foodlook.com
Text: Günter Beer, Gerhard von Richthofen, Patrik Jaros, Jörg Zipprick
Photography: Günter Beer www.beerfoto.com
Photographer's assistants: Sigurd Buchberger, Aranxa Alvarez
Cook's assistants: Magnus Thelen, Johannes von Bemberg
Designed by Estudio Merino www.estudiomerino.com
Produced by Buenavista Studio s.l. www.buenavistastudio.com
The visual index is a registered design of Buenavista Studio s.l. (European Trademark Office number 000252796-001)
Project managment: trans texas publishing, Cologne
Typesetting: Nazire Ergün, Cologne

Notes for the Reader
This book uses standard kitchen measuring spoons and cups. All spoon and cup measurements are level unless otherwise indicated. Unless otherwise stated, milk is assumed to be whole, butter is assumed to be salted, eggs are large, individual vegetables are medium, and pepper is freshly ground black pepper. Unless otherwise stated, all root vegetables should be washed and peeled before using.

Garnishes and serving suggestions are all optional and not necessarily included in the recipe ingredients or method. The times given are only an approximate guide. Preparation times differ according to the techniques used by different people and the cooking times may also vary from those given. Optional ingredients, variations, or serving suggestions have not been included in the calculations.

Recipes using raw or very lightly cooked eggs should be avoided by infants, the elderly, pregnant women, and people with weakened immune systems. Pregnant and breast-feeding women are advised to avoid eating peanuts and peanut products. People with nut allergies should be aware that some of the prepared ingredients used in the recipes in this book may contain nuts. Always check the packaging before use.

Picture acknowledgments
All photos by Günter Beer, Barcelona

Contents

Introduction

Desserts are the culinary climax of a successful meal, the final course that leaves your family and guests feeling pleasantly replete.

The world of desserts is very diverse. From light fruit-based treats and creamy puddings to oven-baked specialties, there is something to suit every taste. The dessert is the last part of a meal and should be chosen with care—after all, it makes the final impression and is the one guests take home with them. It's also important that the dessert complements the rest of the menu. If you remember just a few small points, you should have a success. For example, after heavier dishes, it's advisable to choose lighter, fruity desserts so that your guests are not left feeling too full. If the first courses are less filling, you can serve a more substantial dessert. In the summer, cool fruit and ice cream desserts offer welcome refreshment, while in the fall or winter months, richer, warming desserts will be a treat.

If you choose a certain national cuisine to be the theme of your menu, make sure the dessert complements this choice. For example, it's best to serve a French dessert with a French menu, Wine Chaudeau or Baked Peaches with Lavender, perhaps. An Italian meal can be rounded off with Zabaglione or Panna Cotta. For an Asian meal, on the other hand, Tapioca-Coconut Pudding, Spring Rolls with Cherry Filling or Fried Fine Noodles in Strawberry Gazpacho would make an excellent choice.

Fruit

Fruit-based desserts go with virtually any menu and can be varied in a multitude of ways. They can be refined with exotic fruits, dried fruit, fine sweet sauces (you can find a selection of these on pages 12–13), nuts, or liqueurs, and adapted to all kinds of menus. When using fruit, especially berries, make sure you buy seasonal, local produce whenever possible. They will have more flavor than imported goods. Frozen berries that have been harvested in the appropriate season are also a far better choice than imported produce.

Remember, what applies to every other dish also applies to desserts: the higher the quality of the ingredients, the better the finished dish!

Chocolate

Chocolate desserts are not only favorites with children, they're also a popular choice with adults. To guarantee the perfect chocolate treat, always use superior-quality chocolate. If a recipe specifies bittersweet chocolate, such as Dark Chocolate Mousse, use chocolate with a 70-percent cocoa content. This is more expensive than chocolate with a lower cocoa content, but it's far more intense and gives the dessert a very distinct flavor. Strictly speaking, white chocolate is not really chocolate because it contains cocoa butter instead of cocoa. If using white chocolate—for example, for White Chocolate Mousse with Maple Syrup—buy a product with a high cocoa butter content.

For recipes containing cocoa powder, such as Tiramisù, use an unsweetened, low-fat product. Cocoa should never be substituted with a hot cocoa mix because it does not contain the required amount of cocoa and is far too sweet.

Decoration

In no other course of a menu is decoration as important as it can be for a dessert. This is where you can give your creativity full reign. Fruit, especially berries, makes attractive garnishes, while candied petals, such as violets, roses, or pansies, can turn a simple dessert into a work of art. However, some desserts look good without additional embellishment. In such cases, simply dust with a little confectioners' sugar or unsweetened cocoa powder, or add a few sprigs of fresh herbs, such as lavender, mint, or lemon balm. Other decorations not only look good but will give your dessert additional flavor. This is true of roasted, chopped nuts, chocolate curls and shavings, and the grated zest of citrus fruits. Sweet sauces and syrups can also add a splash of color to desserts and enhance their flavors. Bavarian Cream, for example, is usually served with a fruity sauce. Some desserts, such as ice creams, are often served with one or two home-baked cookies or brownies.

Equipment
You don't necessarily need to buy expensive kitchen gadgets to prepare different desserts, but there are some utensils that will certainly make preparation a lot easier. A good set of kitchen measuring cups and spoons is a worthwhile investment because the quantities stated in recipes need to be observed exactly when making desserts. A good electric mixer is also useful. You will also need a wire whisk to prepare light cream desserts and sauces made over a water bath. Good nonstick baking pans prevent oven-baked desserts from sticking or collapsing when inverted. To make the delicious, low-fat White Chocolate Mousse with Maple Syrup, you will need a siphon.

Buy a pastry bag with interchangeable tips to pipe attractive decorations onto cakes and cream desserts. A chef's blowtorch gives a professional finish to a range of desserts that would otherwise have to be browned under the broiler.

How to use this book

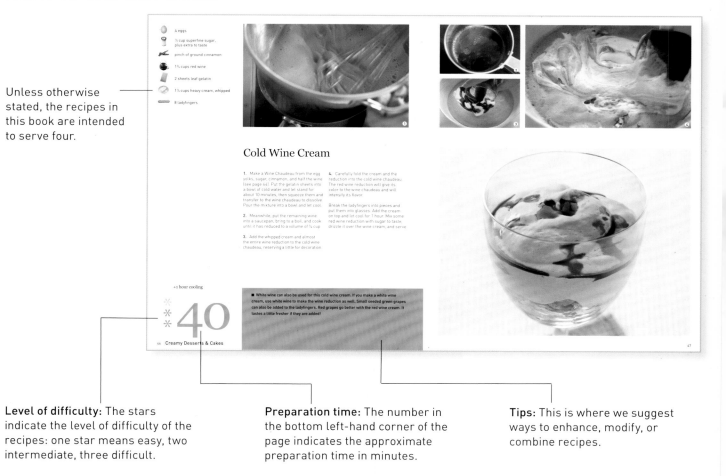

Unless otherwise stated, the recipes in this book are intended to serve four.

Level of difficulty: The stars indicate the level of difficulty of the recipes: one star means easy, two intermediate, three difficult.

Preparation time: The number in the bottom left-hand corner of the page indicates the approximate preparation time in minutes.

Tips: This is where we suggest ways to enhance, modify, or combine recipes.

3¼ cups all-purpose flour

 1¾ sticks unsalted butter, cut into small pieces and chilled

 ½ cup sugar

 pinch of salt

 2 eggs

Sweet Flaky Pastry Dough

1. Place the flour, butter, sugar, and salt on a work surface.

2. Using both hands, quickly rub the butter into the flour. If it is worked for too long, the butter will become warm and the dough will crumble later.

3. Separate one of the eggs. Add one egg and one egg yolk to the flour mixture and work in. Store the remaining egg white in the refrigerator for later use.

4. Knead the dough briskly and thoroughly until it is smooth and elastic.

Wrap in plastic wrap and refrigerate for at least 1 hour.

Makes enough for two 9-inch pie crusts, plus extra for trimmings

75

■ Use this basic recipe to make delicious almond cookies—simply substitute ¾ cup of the flour with 1 cup of finely chopped almonds. Prepare the dough as described above, shape into cookies, and bake until golden brown.

Vanilla Sauce

Cut **1 vanilla bean** in half lengthwise and scrape out the seeds with the back of a knife. Add the seeds and the bean to **1 cup of milk** in a saucepan and bring to a boil. Meanwhile, separate **6 eggs**. Combine the egg yolks with **½ cup of sugar**, and beat until fluffy. Bring some water to a boil in a saucepan, then let simmer. As soon as the milk boils, pour it through a strainer so that none of the vanilla bean is included in the sauce. Gradually add the hot milk to the egg-sugar mixture, stirring continuously. Heat the mixture over the simmering water and stir until it is thick enough to coat the back of a spoon. Place over a bowl of iced water and stir until cold.

■ **If the sauce becomes too hot, it will curdle. If this happens, pass it through a fine strainer. Stir in 1 tablespoon of cornstarch and 2 tablespoons of milk and whisk them into the hot vanilla sauce. Return the sauce to a boil and it will be creamy once again.**

Chocolate Sauce

Slowly bring **½ cup of milk**, **½ cup of cream**, and **½ scraped vanilla bean** to a boil in a saucepan. Chop **4 ounces of semisweet chocolate** and **2 ounces of milk chocolate** into small pieces and add to the milk mixture. Stir slowly with a whisk until the chocolate is melted. Remove from the heat, take out the vanilla bean, and stir in **2 teaspoons of cognac**, **2 tablespoons of sugar**, and **2½ tablespoons of vegetable oil**. Pour the sauce through a fine strainer and serve at room temperature.

■ **Use hazelnut oil in place of the vegetable oil for a nutty flavor.**

Caramel Sauce

Put **¼ cup of sugar** and **½ cup of water** into a small saucepan and bring to a boil over low heat. Simmer until the sugar is golden brown and evenly caramelized. Add another **¼ cup of water** to stop the sugar from browning further. Simmer for about 5 minutes, until the water has evaporated. Add **1 cup of milk**. Cut **1 vanilla bean** in half lengthwise and scrape out the seeds with the back of a knife. Add the bean and the seeds to the milk mixture and bring the mixture to a boil. Meanwhile, separate **6 eggs**. Combine the egg yolks with **2½ tablespoons of sugar** and beat until fluffy. Pour some water into a saucepan and bring to a boil, then let simmer. As soon as the milk boils, pour it through a strainer, so that no lumps are included in the sauce. Gradually add the hot milk to the egg-sugar mixture, stirring continuously. Heat the mixture over the simmering water and stir until it is thick enough to coat the back of a spoon. Place over a bowl of iced water and stir until cold.

Strawberry Sauce

Sprinkle **⅓ cup of confectioners' sugar** over **8 ounces of strawberries**. Add **⅓ cup of water** and puree with an immersion blender to make a thin sauce. Pass the puree through a fine strainer and serve.

Apricot Sauce

Put **5 apricots** into boiling water for 10 seconds, then immediately plunge them into cold water to chill them. Peel and halve the apricots and remove the pits. Put the apricot halves, the juice of **½ lemon**, **⅓ cup of confectioners' sugar**, and **⅓ cup of water** in a bowl and mix with an immersion blender. Pass the mixture through a fine strainer and serve.

Kiwi Sauce

Peel **4 kiwis**, put them in a bowl with **⅓ cup of confectioners' sugar** and **⅓ cup of water**, and mix them with an immersion blender. Pass the mixture through a fine strainer and serve.

■ **Kiwis cannot be used with any dairy products, because they contain an enzyme that would curdle them (just like pineapples do).**

1¾ pounds quark, strained cottage cheese, or mascarpone

 1 cup milk

 ½ cup light cream

 5 eggs

 1 lemon

 3½ tablespoons unsalted butter

 ⅓ cup vanilla sugar

 ¾ cup cornstarch

 pinch of salt

 ⅔ cup sugar

 ½ quantity Sweet Flaky Pastry Dough (see page 10)

①

German Cheesecake

1. Preheat the oven to 425°F. Put the quark in a bowl, add the milk and cream, and mix until smooth. Separate the eggs and put the egg whites in a covered bowl in the refrigerator. Rinse the lemon with hot water, then finely grate the zest. Cut the lemon in half and squeeze the juice into a bowl. Melt the butter in a small saucepan over low heat.

2. Add the egg yolks, melted butter, half the vanilla sugar, the lemon juice, lemon zest, and cornstarch to the quark mixture, and stir with a wire whisk until smooth.

3. Beat the egg whites with the salt and sugar until holding soft peaks, then fold into the quark mixture.

4. Roll out the dough to a thickness of slightly less than ¼ inch, and use to line a 9-inch nonstick springform cake pan. Cut any excess dough from around the edges with a knife. Fill the shell with the quark mixture and smooth the surface. Bake in the preheated oven for about 5 minutes, then remove the cake from the oven. Insert a knife between the crust and the skin on top of the cake and make a cut all along the crust. Return to the oven and bake for another 15 minutes. Remove the cake from the oven, let stand until it has sunk a little, and reduce the oven temperature to 325°F. Return the cake to the oven and bake for another 35 minutes.

5. Remove from the oven, let cool, then take it out of the pan. Serve warm with the remaining vanilla sugar sprinkled on top.

■ German cheesecake tastes especially good warm, but it's harder to cut that way—so be careful! Add ⅓ cup of rum-soaked raisins to the quark batter, if liked.

120

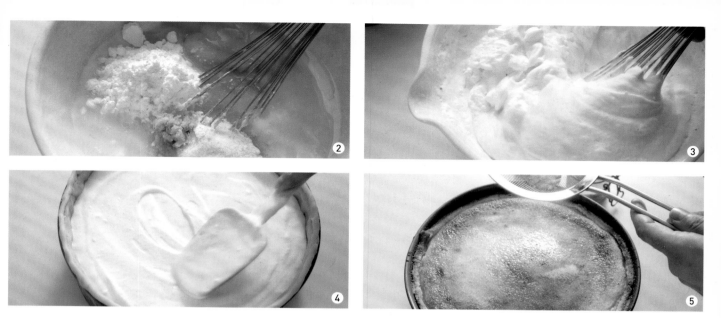

2 cups all-purpose flour

 2 cups milk

 3 tablespoons sugar

 3 eggs

 1¼ sticks butter

 2 tablespoons vegetable oil

Sweet Pancakes

1. Put the flour into a mixing bowl. Add half the milk and the sugar.

2. Whisk the batter until it is smooth and thick.

3. Pour in the remaining milk and beat in the eggs.

4. Melt the butter in a small saucepan until golden brown with a nutty odor.

5. Using the whisk, stir the butter into the batter a little at a time.

6. Heat the oil in a skillet. Using a ladle, pour some batter into the skillet and spread it in a thin layer over the bottom by tilting the skillet back and forth.

7. Using a spatula, loosen the batter from the edge of the skillet and toss the pancake to turn. Alternatively, place a plate upside down over the skillet and invert the skillet so that the pancake falls onto the plate, then return the pancake to the skillet to cook the other side.

8. Cook the pancake briefly after turning. Transfer the cooked pancakes to a plate and let cool before serving.

■ Serve these thin pancakes, or crepes, by spreading them with fresh fruit preserves, or rolling them up, sprinkling them with sugar, and serving with lemon wedges for squeezing over. A fruit filling with Vanilla Sauce (see page 12) is also delicious.

4 eggs

 2 cups confectioners' sugar

 2 cups raspberries, or a mixture of raspberries and blueberries

 2 cups small wild strawberries

 1 cup heavy cream

 seeds of 1 vanilla bean

Meringues with Berries & Vanilla Cream

1. Preheat the oven to 250°F. Separate the eggs and chill the whites in a bowl. Store the egg yolks in the refrigerator for future use. Beat the whites with a wire whisk until holding soft peaks. Gradually add the sugar and beat until stiff.

2. Use a rubber spatula to put the beaten egg whites into a pastry bag.

3. Pipe the egg white mixture into spirals on a baking sheet covered with parchment paper. Bake them in the preheated oven for about 35 minutes, then reduce the temperature to 225°F and let the meringues "dry" for 4 hours.

4. Hull the berries and put them into a bowl.

5. Once cooled, cut the top off the baked meringues with a sharp, serrated knife. Whip the cream with the vanilla seeds and spread the mixture on the lower half of the meringues. Top with berries, set the lids over the berries at an angle, and serve immediately.

+4 hours "drying"

✳
✳
✳
65

■ Try making a miniature version of these meringue cases. They won't take as long to "dry" and can be served as an afternoon treat. They can also be prepared in advance and filled just before they are served. You can also use fruit sorbet as a filling instead of fresh fruit.

6 ounces bittersweet dark chocolate

 2 eggs

 3 tablespoons sugar

 1 tablespoon unsweetened cocoa powder

 1½ tablespoons cognac

 ¼ cup espresso

 pinch of salt

 1 cup heavy cream, whipped

1 cup chocolate shavings, to decorate

Dark Chocolate Mousse

1. Put the chocolate in a heatproof bowl set over a saucepan of barely simmering water.

2. Separate the eggs and chill the egg whites in the refrigerator. Whisk the egg yolks with the sugar until foaming. Stir the cocoa, cognac, and espresso into the egg mixture.

3. Add the warm melted chocolate.

4. Stir until combined.

5. Beat the egg whites with a pinch of salt until holding stiff peaks, then fold them into the chocolate mixture with a wire whisk. Fold in the whipped cream, and let the mousse chill in the refrigerator for at least 2 hours.

To serve, scoop out individual servings and shape with a spoon, then decorate with chocolate shavings.

∗∗160

■ Put a ripe banana into a saucepan with two pieces of finely chopped preserved ginger, the juice of ½ an orange, and ½ a vanilla bean and bring to a boil. Add the mixture as an intermediate layer in the chocolate mousse and let chill in the refrigerator. Chocolate and bananas are an excellent combination and will turn the mousse into a wonderful dessert.

1 envelope powdered gelatin

 3 cups milk

 4 ounces white chocolate

 3 tablespoons maple syrup

White Chocolate Mousse with Maple Syrup

1. Put the gelatin into a glass with ¼ cup of cold water. Stir and let soak for 10 minutes.

2. Heat the milk in a saucepan, then set aside 2 tablespoons. Break the chocolate into pieces, add to the pan, and heat until dissolved.

3. Mix the gelatin with the reserved hot milk, then add to the chocolate-milk mixture and stir until completely dissolved.

4. Pour the chocolate mousse into a siphon with the aid of a funnel.

5. Add the maple syrup, close the siphon when it contains 3 cups of the mixture, and shake well. Let cool in the refrigerator for about 1 hour.

To serve, insert two cartridges and pipe the fluffy mousse into small bowls.

■ The mousse can be prepared in advance using this method. At the last minute, you can serve it fresh in glasses and it will be particularly frothy. Dark chocolate or even fruit purees can be added to the milk. However, fruit purees should not be cooked further and the quantity of gelatin must be increased by half because of the acid in the fruit.

4 eggs

 1/3 cup sugar

 seeds from 1/2 vanilla bean

 2 tablespoons cognac

 1 tablespoon Grand Marnier

 2 cups mascarpone cheese

 14 ladyfingers

 1 cup espresso, cooled

1/2 cup unsweetened cocoa powder

Tiramisu

1. Separate the eggs and store the egg whites in the refrigerator for later use. Beat the yolks with the sugar and the vanilla seeds until fluffy.

2. Add the cognac and Grand Marnier and stir.

3. Using a rubber spatula, add the mascarpone cheese and whisk it into the mixture.

4. Dip the ladyfingers in the espresso for a maximum of 3 seconds, so that they are not completely saturated.

5. Put the ingredients in a bowl in alternating layers. Start with a layer of coffee-soaked ladyfingers, then add a layer of the mascarpone cream and repeat the process. Top with a layer of cream and let chill in the refrigerator for at least 1 hour.

Remove from the refrigerator, sprinkle with the cocoa powder, and serve immediately.

+1 hour cooling

 40

■ If the cream becomes lumpy, add some hot milk and beat it in until the mixture is smooth.

1 freshly made Sponge Sheet Cake (see page 8)

 1 tablespoon sugar

 2 cups strawberries

 1 cup strawberry preserves

Strawberry Jelly Roll

1. Turn out the warm sponge cake onto a sheet of parchment paper sprinkled with sugar. Carefully pull off the top layer of parchment paper.

2. Roll up the sponge cake and let cool. Meanwhile, hull and thinly slice the strawberries.

3. Unroll the sponge cake and spread the strawberry preserves over it. Distribute the sliced strawberries over the spread.

4. Roll up the filled sponge cake, using both hands and applying a light pressure to keep any hollow spaces out of the roll. Let cool for 15 minutes, then cut it into slices about 1 inch thick.

Arrange on a platter and serve.

✳
✳
✳60

■ Rubbing the top sheet of parchment paper with moist paper towels will make it easier to pull it off the top of the sponge cake after it is turned out of the pan.

1 cup milk

 ⅓ cup superfine sugar

 3 eggs, separated

 2½ tablespoons cornstarch

 2 tablespoons unsalted butter

 1 vanilla bean

 1 sheet ready-to-bake puff pastry

 2 cups mixed berries

 3 tablespoons water

 3 tablespoons granulated sugar

 3 tablespoons white wine

 1½ sheets leaf gelatin

 confectioners' sugar, for dusting

 zest of 1 orange, to decorate

Little Fruit Tarts

1. Preheat the oven to 350°F. Mix ¼ cup of the milk with the superfine sugar, 1 egg yolk, and the cornstarch. Cut the butter into small pieces and chill in the refrigerator. Cut the vanilla bean in half lengthwise and scrape out the seeds with the back of a knife. Put the remaining milk into a saucepan with the vanilla seeds and bean and bring to a boil. Pour through a strainer into a clean saucepan and return to the heat. Pour the prepared mixture of milk, egg yolk, sugar, and cornstarch slowly into the hot milk and let thicken.

2. Stir the custard and the chilled butter over a bowl of iced water, cover, and let cool.

3. Cut the pastry into triangles and strips and assemble as shown in the photograph. Lightly beat the remaining egg yolks with a fork and use to brush the pastry. Prick the tart bottoms with a fork.

4. Bake in the preheated oven for 12–15 minutes, then let cool. Fill with the vanilla cream to just below the rim.

5. Top the vanilla cream with berries. Put the water, sugar, and wine into a small saucepan and bring to a boil. Meanwhile, put the gelatin sheets into a bowl of cold water and let soak for 10 minutes. Drain the gelatin, add to the pan, dissolve, and let cool. Coat the berries with the glaze.

Dust the tarts with confectioners' sugar, decorate with a twist of orange zest, and serve.

■ The little tarts can be topped with any kind of berries you like. A large slice of puff pastry with vanilla cream and fresh strawberries is also a delicious alternative to a cake.

75

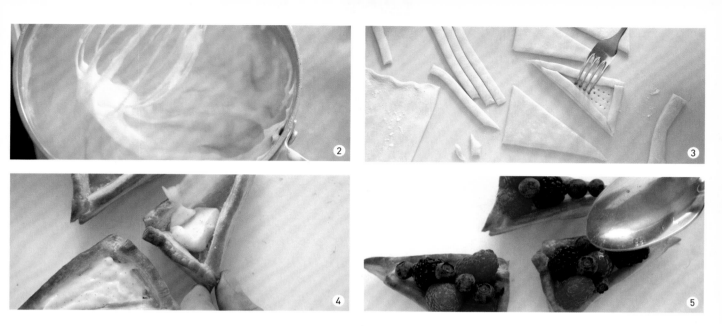

½ vanilla bean

 2 cups cream

 ½ cup sugar

 1 tablespoon coffee beans

 3 sheets leaf gelatin

Coffee Panna Cotta

1. Cut the vanilla bean in half lengthwise. Scrape out the seeds with the back of a knife and add them to the cream. Put the cream into a saucepan with the scraped vanilla bean, sugar, and coffee beans and bring to a boil. Meanwhile, soak the gelatin sheets in cold water for about 10 minutes, until soft.

2. Remove the boiled cream mixture from the heat. Drain the gelatin, add to the hot cream, and let dissolve.

3. Pour the cream through a strainer into a small bowl or large measuring cup.

4. Pour into glasses and let chill in the refrigerator for at least 3 hours until set.

Remove from the refrigerator, put the glasses into hot water for a moment, then turn out the panna cotta and serve.

210

■ Sprinkle the panna cotta with crushed almond cookies or amaretti and decorate it with cherries. For a lighter panna cotta, substitute half of the cream with milk.

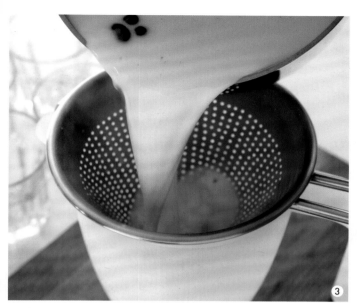

3 eggs

 1¼ cups sugar

 1 tablespoon vanilla sugar

 1¼ cups milk

 1 stick unsalted butter, plus extra for greasing

 2 cups all-purpose flour, plus extra for dusting

 2 teaspoons baking powder

 pinch of salt

 1 teaspoon cornstarch

2 cups red currants or raspberries

2 cups blueberries

Red Berry & Blueberry Meringue Cake

1. Preheat the oven to 350°F. Grease an 11-inch springform cake pan with butter and dust with flour. Separate the eggs and put the whites in the refrigerator. Put the egg yolks into a mixing bowl with ¾ cup of the sugar and the vanilla sugar and beat well. Put the milk and butter into a saucepan and bring to a boil, then add to the sugar-egg mixture and stir well.

2. Sift the flour and the baking powder into the bowl and mix.

3. Pour the cake batter into the prepared pan and bake in the preheated oven for 18 minutes. Remove from the oven and let cool slightly. Increase the oven temperature to 425°F.

4. Using an electric mixer, beat the egg whites, salt, and the remaining sugar until creamy. Add the cornstarch and beat on the highest setting for 1 minute, until holding stiff peaks. Carefully mix the fruit into the egg whites, reserving some of each type of berry.

5. Spread the meringue over the baked cake.

6. Sprinkle the reserved berries over the meringue. Return the cake to the oven and bake for about 15 minutes. Remove from the oven and let cool.

Transfer to a platter to serve.

*** 100**

■ After the cake has cooled, spread 1¼-inch-thick layers of vanilla and chocolate ice cream over it. Cover with the meringue and bake for 5 minutes at 475°F. Remove from the oven and serve immediately.

5 eggs

 8 ladyfingers

 3 tablespoons Grand Marnier

 3 tablespoons butter

 1 vanilla bean

 ¼ cup cornstarch

 1 cup milk

 ½ cup superfine sugar

 pinch of salt

Vanilla Sponge Soufflés

1. Separate the eggs and put 1 egg white in the refrigerator for later use. Cut the ladyfingers into ¼-inch cubes, place in a dish, and pour over the Grand Marnier. Let 2 tablespoons of the butter soften at room temperature. Cut the vanilla bean in half lengthwise and scrape out the seeds with the back of a knife. Beat the four remaining egg whites until holding stiff peaks, cover, and let chill in the refrigerator. Mix the cornstarch with 2½ tablespoons of the milk. Put the remaining milk in a saucepan, add the remaining butter, ⅓ cup of the sugar, the vanilla seeds, vanilla bean, and salt, and bring to a boil.

2. Use a brush to coat four ramekins (individual ceramic dishes) with the softened butter. Line the ramekins by putting some sugar into each of them and tilting, as shown in the photograph, so that some sugar coats the sides and the surplus falls into the bowl.

3. Add the cold milk and the cornstarch to the boiling milk mixture, stirring with a wire whisk continuously for 2 minutes. The cornstarch will thicken the milk. Cover with plastic wrap and let cool. Meanwhile, preheat the oven to 375°F. Line a baking pan with parchment paper, pour in water to a depth of two fingers to make a water bath, and put it in the preheated oven until the water starts to boil.

■ Cover the soufflé mixture with plastic wrap while cooling to prevent a skin from forming. When it comes to service, always have your guests seated before serving—guests wait for a soufflé, but soufflés don't wait for guests.

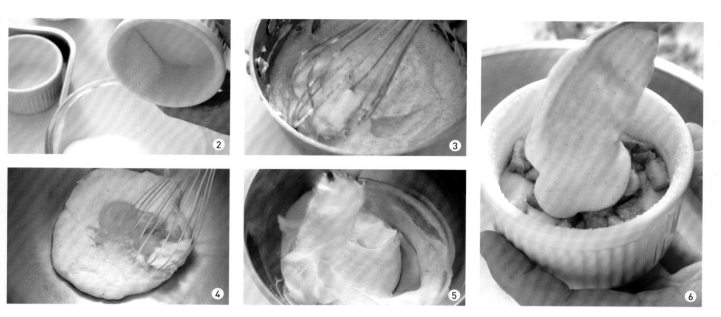

4. Stir the egg yolks into the cooled mixture. It must be cool to prevent the egg from curdling. Pass the mixture through a strainer to remove any lumps.

5. Fold the beaten egg whites carefully into the egg yolk mixture with a rubber spatula. Stir gently so that none of the trapped air escapes. Divide the ladyfinger cubes among the ramekins.

6. Spoon the soufflé mixture on top of the ladyfinger cubes. Place the ramekins in the water bath and bake the soufflés in the preheated oven for 20 minutes. They are cooked when they turn golden yellow and reach a height of ¾–1¼ inches above the rims of the ramekins.

Remove the soufflés from the oven, invert onto individual plates and serve immediately with Chocolate Sauce (see page 12).

2 tablespoons butter, softened, plus extra for greasing

 2½ tablespoons flour

 1 vanilla bean

 ¾ cup walnuts

 1 ounce semisweet dark chocolate

 3 eggs

 ⅓ cup superfine sugar

 1 cup milk

 confectioners' sugar, for dusting

Walnut Soufflés

1. Mix the butter with the flour in a small bowl until it forms a smooth paste. Cut the vanilla bean in half lengthwise and scrape out the seeds with the back of a knife. Coarsely chop the walnuts and the chocolate. Separate the eggs. Beat the egg whites until holding soft peaks, then cover and chill in the refrigerator. Grease four ramekins (individual ceramic dishes) and line the rims with superfine sugar (see Step 2 on page 34).

2. Put the milk, walnuts, chocolate, vanilla seeds, and vanilla bean into a saucepan and bring to a boil. Remove the vanilla bean and stir in the butter-flour paste.

3. Simmer for 3 minutes, stirring continuously, until the mixture thickens. Cover with plastic wrap and let cool. Meanwhile, preheat the oven to 400°F. Pour water into a baking pan to a depth of two fingers to make a water bath. When the mixture has cooled to room temperature, stir in the egg yolks. Gently fold in the beaten egg whites with a rubber spatula. Fill the ramekins two-thirds full with the mixture, put them in the water bath and bake in the water bath for 20 minutes, or until the soufflés have risen ¾ inch above the ramekin rims.

Sprinkle with the confectioners' sugar and serve immediately.

■ You can use this basic recipe to whip up different kinds of soufflés in no time. Just substitute other ingredients for the walnuts. For best results, use hazelnuts, chestnut puree, roasted almonds, or dried coconut. However, if you are using coconut, white chocolate should be substituted for the dark chocolate.

6 eggs

 ½ cup superfine sugar

 1 cup sparkling white wine

 ¼ cup Marsala wine

 juice of ½ lemon

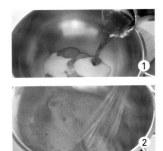 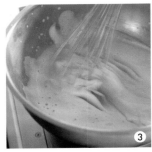 

1. Hot Zabaglione

1. Separate the eggs. Store the egg whites in the refrigerator for future use. Put the egg yolks, sugar, white wine, Marsala wine, and lemon juice into a bowl.

2. Beat the mixture over a saucepan of barely simmering water, scraping the edges of the bowl to avoid lumps being created.

3. The mixture will become lighter in color and more viscous, and will increase in volume.

4. The zabaglione is ready when it has a creamy, glossy consistency.

Pour into glasses and serve immediately.

2. Pistachio Zabaglione

Separate **4 eggs**. Store the egg whites in the refrigerator for future use. Beat the egg yolks with ⅓ **cup of sugar** and ½ **cup of sparkling white wine** over a pan of simmering water, as in the basic zabaglione recipe. Put **1 sheet of leaf gelatin** into warm water, dissolve it, then add it to the zabaglione. Stir this mixture over a bowl of iced water until it is cold. Grind ½ **cup of pistachio nuts** in a blender until they are almost like a paste and add them to the zabaglione. Whip ½ **cup of heavy cream** until holding soft peaks and fold it into the mixture.

Pour the zabaglione into glasses and serve with crushed pistachios sprinkled on top.

3. Campari Zabaglione

Separate **4 eggs**. Store the egg whites in the refrigerator for future use. Beat the egg yolks with ⅓ **cup of sugar** and ⅓ **cup of Campari** in a water bath as in the basic zabaglione recipe. Finely grate some **orange zest** and add to the zabaglione. Heat **1 sheet of leaf gelatin** in the juice of **1 orange** until dissolved and add to the zabaglione. Stir this mixture over a bowl of iced water until cold. Whip ⅓ **cup of heavy cream** until holding soft peaks and fold it in.

Pour the zabaglione into glasses and serve topped with strips of orange zest.

* * * 30

¾ cup superfine sugar

½ cup water

3 eggs

seeds from 1 vanilla bean

2 teaspoons amaretto

2 cups heavy cream

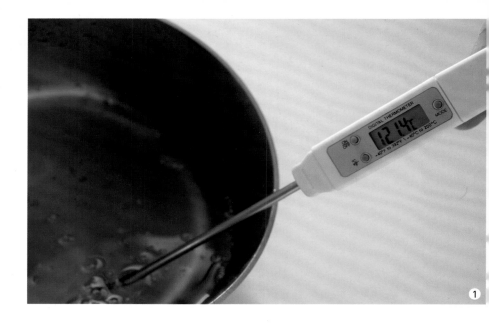

Vanilla Ice Cream Parfait

1. Put the sugar and water in a saucepan and heat to precisely 250°F. Use a candy thermometer to check the temperature.

2. Separate the eggs. Store the egg whites in the refrigerator for future use. Put the egg yolks into a metal bowl. Gradually mix the sugar syrup with the egg yolks, stirring continuously with a wire whisk so that the egg doesn't solidify.

3. Mix in the vanilla seeds and the amaretto, then whisk the mixture until creamy. Stir it over a bowl of iced water until cold.

4. Beat the cream until holding stiff peaks, then stir in one third of the cream with a wire whisk. Carefully fold in the remaining cream.

5. Pour the mixture into a mold and put it in the freezer for at least 6 hours. Hold the mold briefly under hot running hot water to invert the parfait. Use a hot knife to cut ½-inch-thick slices and serve immediately. Wrap any remaining parfait in plastic wrap and store in the freezer.

Variations on the parfait can be made by adding any of the following ingredients:
- 1 cup of strawberry puree
- ¾ cup of passion fruit puree with 3 tablespoons of coconut liqueur
- ½ cup of roasted almonds, ½ cup of coarsely chopped candied cherries, and 2 teaspoons of cherry liqueur
- 1 cup of apricot puree with 2 teaspoons of amaretto

+6 hours freezing

■ You can also surprise your guests with an ice cream soufflé by making a collar from parchment paper, putting it into a miniature soufflé dish, and pouring in some parfait mixture. The parfait creates the effect of a soufflé, but it is made with ice cream.

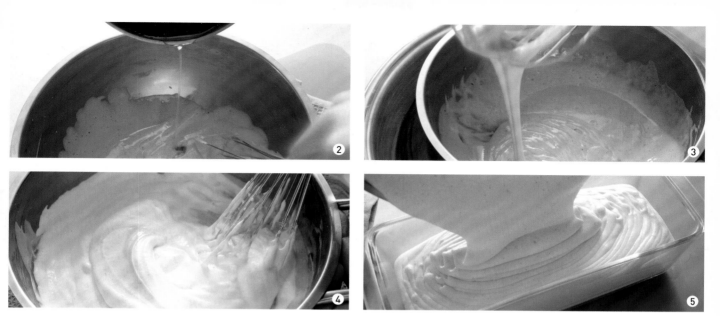

5 eggs

 2/3 cup superfine sugar

 2 cups milk

1 vanilla bean

8 sheets leaf gelatin

1 3/4 cups heavy cream, whipped

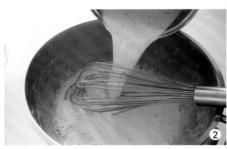

Bavarian Cream

1. Separate the eggs. Store the egg whites in the refrigerator for future use. Whisk the egg yolks with the sugar until the mixture is almost white. Prepare a water bath, being careful that the bowl does not touch the water.

2. Put the milk, vanilla bean, and vanilla seeds into a separate saucepan, bring to a boil, and, using a wire whisk, stir gradually into the egg-sugar mixture.

3. Slowly heat the mixture in the water bath over low heat, stirring continuously with a wooden spoon so that the egg doesn't solidify at the edge of the bowl.

4. Stir the mixture until the egg thickens. The mixture is ready when it coats the back of the wooden spoon.

5. Soften the gelatin sheets in warm water, squeeze them, and then mix them with the whipped cream. Stir over a bowl of iced water until cold.

6. Carefully fold some of the whipped cream into the egg-and-milk mixture and gently mix with a whisk.

*
**
* 40

■ You can also make a coffee cream by adding some espresso to the egg mixture before folding in the cream. Increase the quantity of gelatin sheets to 9.

7. Fold in the remaining cream, turning the whisk with your wrist, as if you were using a stirring spoon. Pour into dishes, cover, and chill in the refrigerator.

Serve the cream with a fruit sauce (see page 13) or fresh fruit.

8 eggs

 1 cup superfine sugar

 ¼ teaspoon ground cinnamon, plus extra for dusting

 3⅓ cups red wine

Wine Chaudeau

1. Separate the eggs. Store the egg whites in the refrigerator for future use. Put the egg yolks into a stainless steel bowl. Add the sugar and the cinnamon.

2. Pour in the wine and mix it in with a wire whisk. Fill a saucepan ¾-inch deep with water and bring to a boil over high heat.

3. Place the bowl over the saucepan.

4. Beat the mixture vigorously until the volume increases three-fold and the custard is thick and creamy.

Remove from the heat and pour into glasses. Serve hot, with some cinnamon sprinkled on top.

■ Hot red wine chaudeau is especially delicious when served with baked pears, peaches, or apples. If you substitute Prosecco or Marsala wine for the red wine, you will produce a mouthwatering zabaglione.

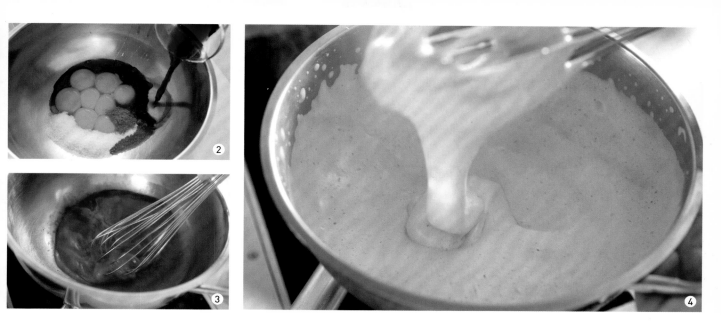

4 eggs

 ½ cup superfine sugar, plus extra to taste

 pinch of ground cinnamon

 1¾ cups red wine

 2 sheets leaf gelatin

 1¼ cups heavy cream, whipped

 8 ladyfingers

Cold Wine Cream

1. Make a Wine Chaudeau from the egg yolks, sugar, cinnamon, and half the wine (see page 44). Put the gelatin sheets into a bowl of cold water and let stand for about 10 minutes, then squeeze them and transfer to the wine chaudeau to dissolve. Pour the mixture into a bowl and let cool.

2. Meanwhile, put the remaining wine into a saucepan, bring to a boil, and cook until it has reduced to a volume of ¼ cup.

3. Add the whipped cream and almost the entire wine reduction to the cold wine chaudeau, reserving a little for decoration.

4. Carefully fold the cream and the reduction into the cold wine chaudeau. The red wine reduction will give its color to the wine chaudeau and will intensify its flavor.

Break the ladyfingers into pieces and put them into glasses. Add the cream on top and let cool for 1 hour. Mix some red wine reduction with sugar to taste, drizzle it over the wine cream, and serve.

+1 hour cooling

* * * 40

■ White wine can also be used for this cold wine cream. If you make a white wine cream, use white wine to make the wine reduction as well. Small seeded green grapes can also be added to the ladyfingers. Red grapes go better with the red wine cream. It tastes a little fresher if they are added!

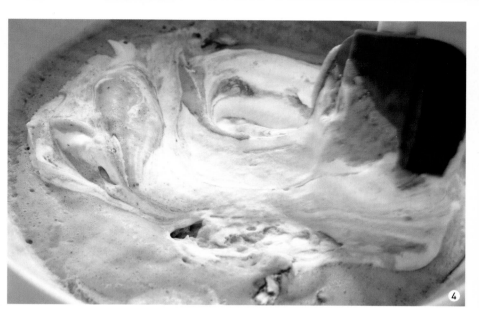

2½ cups coconut milk

 1 cup tapioca flour

 ⅓ cup raw brown sugar

 1 vanilla bean

 pinch of salt

 ½ cup orange juice

 3 star anise

 1 tablespoon granulated sugar

 1 tablespoon cornstarch

 1½ tablespoons orange liqueur

 2 oranges

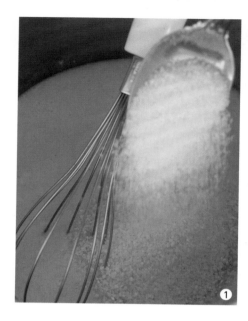

Tapioca-Coconut Pudding

1. Put the coconut milk into a saucepan and bring to a boil. Slowly sprinkle in the tapioca and stir with a wire whisk.

2. Add the raw brown sugar and simmer for 5 minutes. Scrape out the vanilla bean and add the vanilla seeds and the salt.

3. The pudding is cooked once it has a firm, even consistency. Pour it into glasses or bowls, cover with plastic wrap, and let cool.

4. Put the orange juice, star anise, and granulated sugar into a small saucepan and bring to a boil.

5. Mix the cornstarch with the orange liqueur and add to the orange juice mixture to thicken.

6. Peel and segment the oranges and add the slices to the thickened sauce. Remove the sauce from the heat and let cool.

Pour the sauce over the tapioca pudding and serve.

■ The coconut milk must not be thickened. If the pudding sticks to the bottom of the pan, stop stirring and pour it out right away. Green tea ice cream or stewed papaya are perfect accompaniments to this pudding.

 8 ladyfingers

 2 cups cherries,
plus extra to serve

 2 tablespoons granulated sugar

 ½ teaspoon ground cinnamon

 1½ tablespoons cherry liqueur

 1 package spring roll wrappers
(about 4½ × 4½ inches)

 1 egg white, for brushing

 9 cups vegetable oil,
for deep-frying

 confectioners' sugar, for dusting

Spring Rolls with Cherry Filling

1. Put the ladyfingers into a bowl and crush.

2. Halve and pit the cherries and add to the ladyfingers.

3. Add the sugar and the cinnamon.

4. Drizzle with the cherry liqueur and mix well.

5. Lay the spring roll wrappers on the work surface. Put 2 tablespoons of the cherry filling in the center of each. Brush the edges with egg white.

6. Fold two opposite corners into the center and brush the edges with egg white.

7. Fold in the third corner and brush the lower section with egg white.

8. Fold the lower section onto the filling and press down lightly. Brush the upper section with egg white and roll up the wrap completely.

9. Put the oil in a large saucepan and heat to 325°F. Add the spring rolls and deep-fry for about 5 minutes, or until they are golden.

10. Remove the spring rolls and drain on paper towels.

Arrange the spring rolls on plates, sprinkle with confectioners' sugar, and serve with whole cherries.

■ These spring rolls can also be filled with other fruit, such as plums, bananas, mangoes, or grapes. Filling with vanilla cream is also an option, although you will need to use some soaked broken ladyfingers to give the filling structure.

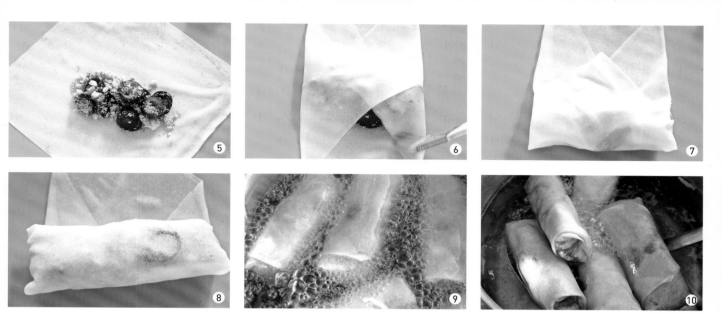

1 stick butter, softened

 ⅓ cup firmly packed light brown sugar

 3 eggs

 ½ cup slivered almonds

 2 cups fresh white bread crumbs

 4 peaches

 8 fresh lavender sprigs, plus extra to decorate

 1 vanilla bean

 4 teaspoons honey

 3 tablespoons peach liqueur

Baked Peaches with Lavender

1. Preheat the oven to 425°F. Put the butter and the sugar into a mixing bowl and beat until fluffy. Separate the eggs. Store the egg whites in the refrigerator for future use. Gradually beat the yolks into the mixture.

2. Toast the slivered almonds in a skillet until golden, then let cool. Add the almonds and the bread crumbs to the butter-egg mixture and mix well.

3. Score the peach skins lightly with a knife, then put the fruit into a heatproof bowl, pour over boiling water, and let stand for 10–15 seconds. Remove the peaches with a slotted spoon and place them in iced water to cool.

4. Remove the skins and cut the peaches in half. Lay the lavender sprigs in the bottom of a baking dish. Remove the peach pits and put the peach halves, cut side up, on top of the lavender sprigs.

5. Fill the peaches with the almond mixture. Cut the vanilla bean in half lengthwise and divide it into 1¼-inch lengths. Drizzle the peaches with the honey and the peach liqueur and bake in the preheated oven for about 20 minutes.

Arrange the peaches on plates, decorate with the vanilla strips and lavender sprigs, and serve.

■ For baked apples with raisin filling, use 3 tablespoons of fluffy whipped butter, ½ cup of lightly toasted, chopped almonds, ⅓ cup of raisins (softened in 2 tablespoons of tea), 1¾ slices of crustless white bread, cut into cubes, 2 ounces of marzipan, 8 small red apples with stems, 1 tablespoon of sugar, 1 tablespoon of honey, 5 cloves, and 2 cinnamon sticks. Prepare these ingredients in the same way as in the baked peaches recipe and cook for the same length of time.

1 pound strawberries

 10 fresh mint leaves

 ½ teaspoon green peppercorns

 3 tablespoons confectioners' sugar

 2½ cups water

 4 cups vegetable oil

 8 ounces fine noodles

Fried Fine Noodles in Strawberry Gazpacho

1. Hull and halve the strawberries, reserving two to decorate, and put them into a bowl. Add the mint leaves and the peppercorns.

2. Add 2 tablespoons of the sugar.

3. Pour in the water and mix, then transfer to a food processor and puree. Pour the puree into a bowl and let cool in the refrigerator for about 1 hour.

4. Heat the oil to 325°F in a small heavy saucepan. Using scissors, cut the noodles in four, add to the pan in batches, and fry for a few seconds.

5. Drain the fried noodles on paper towels and sprinkle them with the remaining sugar while still warm.

Pour the gazpacho into chilled bowls and top with the noodles. Halve the reserved strawberries and place one half in each bowl. Serve immediately, before the noodles absorb the liquid.

■ Watermelon, flavored with a little vodka, can be used instead of strawberries.

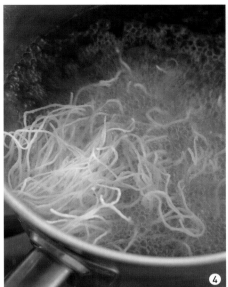

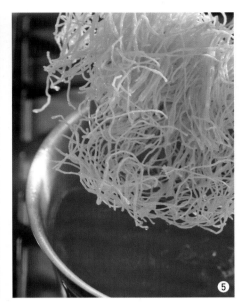

1 tablespoon lemon juice

 ½ cup low-fat Greek-style yogurt

 ½ cup crème fraîche or sour cream

 ¾ cup confectioners' sugar

 ½ cup strawberry puree

 4 sheets leaf gelatin

 ½ cup heavy cream

 2 eggs

 ¼ cup granulated sugar

 3 strawberries, hulled and sliced, to decorate

Strawberry Yogurt Mousse

1. Combine the lemon juice with the yogurt, crème fraîche, confectioners' sugar, and two thirds of the strawberry puree. Place the gelatin sheets in a bowl of cold water and let soak for 10 minutes, then squeeze out the moisture, transfer to a small saucepan, and let dissolve. Mix the gelatin with the yogurt mixture.

2. Whip the cream until holding stiff peaks and then fold carefully into the mixture with a wire whisk.

3. Separate the eggs. Store the egg yolks in the refrigerator for future use. Put the egg whites into a bowl, add the granulated sugar, and beat until holding stiff peaks. Slowly fold them into the mixture.

Pour the mixture into glasses and chill in the refrigerator for 1 hour. Add a little of the remaining strawberry puree to each glass, decorate with the strawberry slices, and serve.

120

3 bananas (about 1 pound),
peeled, plus extra to decorate

juice of 2 lemons

¼ cup banana liqueur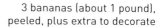

2 tablespoons butter

2½ sheets leaf gelatin

½ cup heavy cream

2 eggs

⅓ cup sugar

2 teaspoon vanilla sugar

¼ cup Chocolate Sauce
(see page 12), to serve

Banana Mousse

1. Thinly slice the bananas, then drizzle with lemon juice to prevent discoloration. Put the bananas, banana liqueur, and butter into a saucepan and bring to a boil. Puree with an immersion blender and strain through a strainer. Place the gelatin sheets in a bowl of cold water and let soak for 10 minutes, then squeeze out the moisture, transfer to a small saucepan, and let dissolve. Stir into the banana puree and let cool.

2. Whip the cream until holding soft peaks, then fold carefully into the chilled banana puree.

3. Separate the eggs. Store the egg yolks in the refrigerator for future use. Put the egg whites into a bowl and beat until they are light and fluffy, then carefully add the sugar and vanilla sugar. Beat until holding stiff peaks, then fold into the mousse and pour into individual glasses. Chill in the refrigerator for at least 2 hours.

Decorate with some unpeeled banana slices and drizzle chocolate sauce on top.

160

* * *

2¼ sticks unsalted butter

 2¼ cups sugar

 ¼ cup vanilla sugar

 4 eggs

 2 cups unsweetened cocoa powder

 2 cups all-purpose flour, sifted

 1 teaspoon baking powder

 pinch of salt

 1½ cups almond meal (ground almonds)

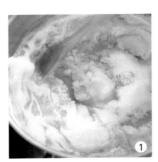  

Chocolate Brownies

1. Preheat the oven to 350°F. Slowly melt the butter in a wide saucepan. Add the sugar and vanilla sugar and mix. Remove from the heat and stir in the eggs one at a time.

2. Add the cocoa powder and stir with a whisk, then add the flour, baking powder, salt, and almond meal, mixing until smooth.

3. Pour the mixture into a nonstick baking pan and smooth the surface. Bake in the preheated oven for about 35 minutes. Remove from the oven and let cool. Invert out of the pan and cut into 1½-inch squares.

Serve warm, with a scoop of vanilla ice cream, if liked.

■ For a more intense chocolate flavor, chop some dark chocolate and stir it into the brownie batter.

 **60**

½ cup firmly packed light brown sugar

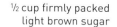
2¼ sticks unsalted butter

2 cups granulated sugar

2 tablespoons vanilla sugar

2 cups walnuts

4 eggs, beaten

2 cups unsweetened cocoa powder

1¾ cups all-purpose flour

1 teaspoon baking powder

pinch of salt

Walnut Caramel Brownies

1. Preheat the oven to 350°F. Put the brown sugar into a wide saucepan over medium heat and heat until caramelized. Add ½ cup cold water and dissolve the caramelized sugar. Add the butter and heat until melted, then remove the pan from the heat. Add the granulated sugar and vanilla sugar and mix. Coarsely chop three-quarters of the walnuts and set aside.

2. Gradually stir in the eggs, then add the cocoa powder. Sift together the flour, baking powder, and salt into the mixture. Add the chopped walnuts and mix.

3. Spread the mixture over the bottom of a nonstick baking pan and smooth the surface. Add the remaining walnuts. Bake in the preheated oven for about 35 minutes. Remove from the oven and let cool.

Invert out of the pan and cut into 1½-inch squares. Serve warm, with a scoop of vanilla ice cream, if liked.

■ Brownies also taste good with a variety of other nuts, such as macadamia nuts, pecans, or Brazil nuts.

60

1 quantity Sweet Flaky Pastry Dough (see page 10)

 flour, for dusting

 ½ cup fruit jelly, jam, or other preserves, such as raspberry, strawberry, or apricot

 1 tablespoon confectioners' sugar, to decorate

Jelly-Filled Cookies

1. Preheat the oven to 400°F. Roll out the dough on a lightly floured work surface to a thickness of slightly less than ⅛ inch. Flip the dough continuously as you roll, sprinkling more flour each time so that it doesn't stick to the work surface.

2. Cut out shapes from the dough with cookie cutters.

3. Lay a piece of parchment paper in a baking sheet, then arrange the shapes on the sheet. Bake in the preheated oven for 8–10 minutes.

4. Remove the cookies from the baking sheet and let cool. Spread the jelly or other preserves on half the cookies.

5. Place the remaining cookies on top to make a sandwich.

Sprinkle with confectioners' sugar and arrange on a plate to serve.

■ If you don't have any cookie cutters, use the rim of a glass.

1 stick unsalted butter

 ¾ cup confectioners' sugar

 ⅓ cup granulated sugar

 ½ teaspoon salt

 1½ cups pecan nuts

 1⅓ cups all-purpose flour

 1 teaspoon baking powder

 1 egg

 cornstarch, for dusting

Butter Pecan Cookies

1. On a work surface, rub the butter into the confectioners' sugar, granulated sugar, and the salt with your hands, working quickly so the butter doesn't get too warm. Finely grind half the pecan nuts, then coarsely chop the remainder.

2. Sift together the flour and baking powder into the butter mixture and work in. Mix the ground and chopped nuts into the dough.

3. Add the egg and knead, again working quickly so the butter doesn't get too soft and the dough doesn't become sticky.

4. Dust your hands with flour and roll the dough into a 2-inch diameter roll. Cover with plastic wrap and chill in the refrigerator for 1 hour.

5. Meanwhile, preheat the oven to 350°F. Lay a piece of parchment paper on the bottom of a baking sheet. Cut the dough into ¾-inch-thick slices and spread them out on the sheet, leaving a little space between them to allow for spreading. Bake in the preheated oven for about 20 minutes, until golden. Remove from the oven and let cool. They can be stored for several days in an airtight container.

Serve with cold milk, fresh coffee, or hot chocolate.

■ For chocolate cookies, work 8 ounces of chopped semisweet dark chocolate or white chocolate into the dough with the nuts, then bake as directed.

INDEX